50 Light and Refreshing Summer Salads

By: Kelly Johnson

Table of Contents

- Watermelon Feta Salad
- Caprese Salad
- Cucumber Tomato Salad
- Greek Salad
- Quinoa Tabbouleh
- Spinach Strawberry Salad
- Chickpea Salad
- Avocado Citrus Salad
- Summer Corn Salad
- Berry Spinach Salad
- Mango Black Bean Salad
- Asian Cabbage Salad
- Roasted Beet Salad
- Arugula and Peach Salad
- Pesto Pasta Salad
- Grilled Vegetable Salad
- Citrus Kale Salad
- Tomato Basil Salad
- Zucchini Noodle Salad
- Shrimp Avocado Salad
- Lentil Salad with Mint
- Thai Chicken Salad
- Berry Quinoa Salad
- Mediterranean Chickpea Salad
- Roasted Sweet Potato Salad
- Broccoli Salad with Raisins
- Mixed Greens with Berries
- Crab and Avocado Salad
- Farro Salad with Vegetables
- Green Bean and Potato Salad
- Cabbage Slaw with Apples
- Tropical Fruit Salad
- Cucumber Dill Salad
- Roasted Cauliflower Salad
- Spinach and Goat Cheese Salad

- Grilled Peach Salad
- Apple Walnut Salad
- Egg and Avocado Salad
- Panzanella Salad
- Creamy Coleslaw
- Italian Pasta Salad
- Mediterranean Orzo Salad
- Cold Soba Noodle Salad
- Chickpea Tabbouleh
- Antipasto Salad
- Avocado and Bean Salad
- Shrimp and Mango Salad
- Quinoa and Black Bean Salad
- Sweet Potato and Kale Salad
- Mediterranean Couscous Salad

Watermelon Feta Salad

Ingredients:

- 4 cups watermelon, cubed
- 1 cup feta cheese, crumbled
- 1/4 cup fresh mint leaves, chopped
- 2 tablespoons olive oil
- Juice of 1 lime
- Salt and pepper, to taste

Instructions:

1. In a large bowl, combine watermelon, feta cheese, and mint leaves.
2. Drizzle with olive oil and lime juice, then season with salt and pepper.
3. Toss gently to combine and serve immediately.

Caprese Salad

Ingredients:

- 4 ripe tomatoes, sliced
- 250g (8 oz) fresh mozzarella cheese, sliced
- Fresh basil leaves
- 2 tablespoons olive oil
- Balsamic glaze (optional)
- Salt and pepper, to taste

Instructions:

1. On a serving platter, alternate slices of tomatoes and mozzarella cheese.
2. Tuck basil leaves in between the layers.
3. Drizzle with olive oil and balsamic glaze, then season with salt and pepper.

Cucumber Tomato Salad

Ingredients:

- 2 cups cucumbers, diced
- 2 cups tomatoes, diced
- 1/2 red onion, thinly sliced
- 1/4 cup fresh parsley, chopped
- 3 tablespoons olive oil
- 2 tablespoons red wine vinegar
- Salt and pepper, to taste

Instructions:

1. In a large bowl, combine cucumbers, tomatoes, red onion, and parsley.
2. In a separate bowl, whisk together olive oil, red wine vinegar, salt, and pepper.
3. Pour the dressing over the salad and toss to combine.

Greek Salad

Ingredients:

- 2 cups cucumbers, diced
- 2 cups tomatoes, diced
- 1 cup bell peppers, chopped
- 1/2 red onion, sliced
- 1 cup Kalamata olives
- 200g (7 oz) feta cheese, crumbled
- 3 tablespoons olive oil
- 1 tablespoon red wine vinegar
- Oregano, to taste
- Salt and pepper, to taste

Instructions:

1. In a large bowl, combine cucumbers, tomatoes, bell peppers, red onion, olives, and feta cheese.
2. In a small bowl, whisk together olive oil, red wine vinegar, oregano, salt, and pepper.
3. Drizzle the dressing over the salad and toss gently to combine.

Quinoa Tabbouleh

Ingredients:

- 1 cup quinoa, rinsed
- 2 cups water
- 1 cup parsley, finely chopped
- 1/2 cup mint leaves, finely chopped
- 1 cup tomatoes, diced
- 1/2 cucumber, diced
- 1/4 cup olive oil
- Juice of 1 lemon
- Salt and pepper, to taste

Instructions:

1. In a saucepan, combine quinoa and water. Bring to a boil, then reduce heat, cover, and simmer for 15 minutes until quinoa is cooked. Let cool.
2. In a large bowl, combine cooked quinoa, parsley, mint, tomatoes, and cucumber.
3. In a small bowl, whisk together olive oil, lemon juice, salt, and pepper. Pour over the salad and toss to combine.

Spinach Strawberry Salad

Ingredients:

- 4 cups fresh spinach leaves
- 2 cups strawberries, sliced
- 1/2 cup walnuts, chopped
- 1/4 cup feta cheese, crumbled
- 3 tablespoons balsamic vinaigrette

Instructions:

1. In a large bowl, combine spinach, strawberries, walnuts, and feta cheese.
2. Drizzle with balsamic vinaigrette and toss gently to combine. Serve immediately.

Chickpea Salad

Ingredients:

- 1 can (400g) chickpeas, rinsed and drained
- 1 cup cherry tomatoes, halved
- 1/2 cucumber, diced
- 1/4 red onion, diced
- 1/4 cup parsley, chopped
- 3 tablespoons olive oil
- Juice of 1 lemon
- Salt and pepper, to taste

Instructions:

1. In a large bowl, combine chickpeas, cherry tomatoes, cucumber, red onion, and parsley.
2. In a small bowl, whisk together olive oil, lemon juice, salt, and pepper.
3. Pour the dressing over the salad and toss to combine.

Avocado Citrus Salad

Ingredients:

- 2 avocados, diced
- 2 cups mixed greens
- 1 cup orange segments
- 1/2 red onion, thinly sliced
- 1/4 cup walnuts, chopped
- 3 tablespoons olive oil
- Juice of 1 lime
- Salt and pepper, to taste

Instructions:

1. In a large bowl, combine avocados, mixed greens, orange segments, red onion, and walnuts.
2. In a small bowl, whisk together olive oil, lime juice, salt, and pepper.
3. Drizzle the dressing over the salad and toss gently to combine.

Summer Corn Salad

Ingredients:

- 4 cups fresh corn kernels (about 6 ears)
- 1 cup cherry tomatoes, halved
- 1/2 red onion, finely chopped
- 1/4 cup fresh cilantro, chopped
- 1/4 cup lime juice
- 3 tablespoons olive oil
- Salt and pepper, to taste

Instructions:

1. In a large bowl, combine corn, cherry tomatoes, red onion, and cilantro.
2. In a small bowl, whisk together lime juice, olive oil, salt, and pepper.
3. Pour the dressing over the salad and toss to combine. Serve chilled or at room temperature.

Berry Spinach Salad

Ingredients:

- 4 cups fresh spinach leaves
- 1 cup mixed berries (strawberries, blueberries, raspberries)
- 1/2 cup walnuts, toasted
- 1/4 cup feta cheese, crumbled
- 3 tablespoons balsamic vinaigrette

Instructions:

1. In a large bowl, combine spinach, mixed berries, walnuts, and feta cheese.
2. Drizzle with balsamic vinaigrette and toss gently to combine. Serve immediately.

Mango Black Bean Salad

Ingredients:

- 1 can (400g) black beans, rinsed and drained
- 1 ripe mango, diced
- 1 red bell pepper, diced
- 1/4 cup red onion, finely chopped
- 1/4 cup fresh cilantro, chopped
- 2 tablespoons lime juice
- Salt and pepper, to taste

Instructions:

1. In a large bowl, combine black beans, mango, red bell pepper, red onion, and cilantro.
2. Drizzle with lime juice and season with salt and pepper. Toss to combine. Serve chilled or at room temperature.

Asian Cabbage Salad

Ingredients:

- 4 cups shredded cabbage (green and/or purple)
- 1 cup shredded carrots
- 1/2 cup green onions, sliced
- 1/4 cup sesame seeds, toasted
- 1/4 cup rice vinegar
- 3 tablespoons soy sauce
- 2 tablespoons olive oil
- 1 tablespoon honey
- Salt and pepper, to taste

Instructions:

1. In a large bowl, combine cabbage, carrots, green onions, and sesame seeds.
2. In a small bowl, whisk together rice vinegar, soy sauce, olive oil, honey, salt, and pepper.
3. Pour the dressing over the salad and toss to combine.

Roasted Beet Salad

Ingredients:

- 4 medium beets, roasted and diced
- 4 cups mixed greens
- 1/2 cup goat cheese, crumbled
- 1/4 cup walnuts, toasted
- 3 tablespoons balsamic vinaigrette

Instructions:

1. In a large bowl, combine roasted beets, mixed greens, goat cheese, and walnuts.
2. Drizzle with balsamic vinaigrette and toss gently to combine. Serve immediately.

Arugula and Peach Salad

Ingredients:

- 4 cups arugula
- 2 ripe peaches, sliced
- 1/4 cup feta cheese, crumbled
- 1/4 cup walnuts, toasted
- 2 tablespoons olive oil
- Juice of 1 lemon
- Salt and pepper, to taste

Instructions:

1. In a large bowl, combine arugula, peaches, feta cheese, and walnuts.
2. Drizzle with olive oil and lemon juice, then season with salt and pepper. Toss gently to combine and serve immediately.

Pesto Pasta Salad

Ingredients:

- 3 cups cooked pasta (e.g., fusilli or rotini)
- 1 cup cherry tomatoes, halved
- 1/2 cup mozzarella balls, halved
- 1/4 cup pesto sauce
- 1/4 cup fresh basil, chopped
- Salt and pepper, to taste

Instructions:

1. In a large bowl, combine cooked pasta, cherry tomatoes, mozzarella, and pesto sauce.
2. Toss gently to combine, then season with salt and pepper. Serve chilled or at room temperature.

Grilled Vegetable Salad

Ingredients:

- 2 zucchinis, sliced
- 1 red bell pepper, sliced
- 1 yellow bell pepper, sliced
- 1 red onion, sliced
- 3 tablespoons olive oil
- Salt and pepper, to taste
- 2 cups mixed greens
- Balsamic vinaigrette, for serving

Instructions:

1. Preheat the grill to medium heat. Toss sliced vegetables with olive oil, salt, and pepper.
2. Grill vegetables until tender and slightly charred, about 5-7 minutes.
3. In a large bowl, combine grilled vegetables with mixed greens. Drizzle with balsamic vinaigrette before serving.

Citrus Kale Salad

Ingredients:

- 4 cups kale, stems removed and leaves chopped
- 1 cup citrus segments (orange, grapefruit, etc.)
- 1/4 cup red onion, thinly sliced
- 1/4 cup almonds, sliced
- 3 tablespoons olive oil
- Juice of 1 lemon
- Salt and pepper, to taste

Instructions:

1. In a large bowl, massage the kale with olive oil and lemon juice until tender.
2. Add citrus segments, red onion, and almonds.
3. Season with salt and pepper, toss to combine, and serve immediately.

Tomato Basil Salad

Ingredients:

- 4 cups ripe tomatoes, diced
- 1 cup fresh basil leaves, torn
- 1/4 cup red onion, thinly sliced
- 2 tablespoons olive oil
- 1 tablespoon balsamic vinegar
- Salt and pepper, to taste

Instructions:

1. In a large bowl, combine tomatoes, basil, and red onion.
2. Drizzle with olive oil and balsamic vinegar, then season with salt and pepper.
3. Toss gently to combine and serve immediately.

Zucchini Noodle Salad

Ingredients:

- 4 medium zucchinis, spiralized
- 1 cup cherry tomatoes, halved
- 1/2 cup bell pepper, diced
- 1/4 cup parsley, chopped
- 3 tablespoons olive oil
- Juice of 1 lemon
- Salt and pepper, to taste

Instructions:

1. In a large bowl, combine spiralized zucchini, cherry tomatoes, bell pepper, and parsley.
2. Drizzle with olive oil and lemon juice, then season with salt and pepper.
3. Toss gently to combine and serve immediately.

Shrimp Avocado Salad

Ingredients:

- 1 pound cooked shrimp, peeled and deveined
- 2 ripe avocados, diced
- 1 cup cherry tomatoes, halved
- 1/4 cup red onion, finely chopped
- 2 tablespoons lime juice
- 2 tablespoons olive oil
- Salt and pepper, to taste

Instructions:

1. In a large bowl, combine shrimp, avocados, cherry tomatoes, and red onion.
2. Drizzle with lime juice and olive oil, then season with salt and pepper.
3. Toss gently to combine and serve immediately.

Lentil Salad with Mint

Ingredients:

- 1 cup cooked lentils
- 1 cup cucumber, diced
- 1/2 cup cherry tomatoes, halved
- 1/4 cup red onion, finely chopped
- 1/4 cup fresh mint leaves, chopped
- 3 tablespoons olive oil
- Juice of 1 lemon
- Salt and pepper, to taste

Instructions:

1. In a large bowl, combine lentils, cucumber, cherry tomatoes, red onion, and mint.
2. Drizzle with olive oil and lemon juice, then season with salt and pepper.
3. Toss gently to combine and serve chilled or at room temperature.

Thai Chicken Salad

Ingredients:

- 2 cups cooked chicken, shredded
- 2 cups mixed greens
- 1 cup carrots, shredded
- 1/2 cup red cabbage, shredded
- 1/4 cup cilantro, chopped
- 3 tablespoons peanut dressing

Instructions:

1. In a large bowl, combine chicken, mixed greens, carrots, red cabbage, and cilantro.
2. Drizzle with peanut dressing and toss to combine. Serve immediately.

Berry Quinoa Salad

Ingredients:

- 1 cup cooked quinoa
- 1 cup mixed berries (strawberries, blueberries, raspberries)
- 1/4 cup almonds, chopped
- 1/4 cup mint leaves, chopped
- 3 tablespoons honey
- 2 tablespoons lemon juice

Instructions:

1. In a large bowl, combine quinoa, mixed berries, almonds, and mint.
2. In a small bowl, whisk together honey and lemon juice.
3. Drizzle the dressing over the salad and toss gently to combine. Serve immediately.

Mediterranean Chickpea Salad

Ingredients:

- 1 can (400g) chickpeas, rinsed and drained
- 1 cup cherry tomatoes, halved
- 1/2 cucumber, diced
- 1/4 red onion, finely chopped
- 1/4 cup feta cheese, crumbled
- 1/4 cup parsley, chopped
- 3 tablespoons olive oil
- Juice of 1 lemon
- Salt and pepper, to taste

Instructions:

1. In a large bowl, combine chickpeas, cherry tomatoes, cucumber, red onion, feta cheese, and parsley.
2. Drizzle with olive oil and lemon juice, then season with salt and pepper.
3. Toss gently to combine and serve chilled or at room temperature.

Roasted Sweet Potato Salad

Ingredients:

- 2 large sweet potatoes, cubed
- 2 tablespoons olive oil
- Salt and pepper, to taste
- 4 cups mixed greens
- 1/4 cup red onion, thinly sliced
- 1/4 cup feta cheese, crumbled
- 1/4 cup pecans, chopped
- 2 tablespoons balsamic vinaigrette

Instructions:

1. Preheat the oven to 425°F (220°C). Toss sweet potatoes with olive oil, salt, and pepper, and spread on a baking sheet. Roast for 25-30 minutes or until tender.
2. In a large bowl, combine mixed greens, roasted sweet potatoes, red onion, feta cheese, and pecans.
3. Drizzle with balsamic vinaigrette and toss gently to combine. Serve warm or at room temperature.

Broccoli Salad with Raisins

Ingredients:

- 4 cups broccoli florets
- 1/2 cup raisins
- 1/4 cup red onion, finely chopped
- 1/4 cup sunflower seeds
- 1/2 cup Greek yogurt
- 2 tablespoons apple cider vinegar
- 2 tablespoons honey
- Salt and pepper, to taste

Instructions:

1. In a large bowl, combine broccoli, raisins, red onion, and sunflower seeds.
2. In a small bowl, whisk together Greek yogurt, apple cider vinegar, honey, salt, and pepper.
3. Pour the dressing over the broccoli mixture and toss to combine. Serve chilled or at room temperature.

Mixed Greens with Berries

Ingredients:

- 4 cups mixed greens
- 1 cup mixed berries (strawberries, blueberries, raspberries)
- 1/4 cup walnuts, chopped
- 1/4 cup goat cheese, crumbled
- 3 tablespoons balsamic vinaigrette

Instructions:

1. In a large bowl, combine mixed greens, berries, walnuts, and goat cheese.
2. Drizzle with balsamic vinaigrette and toss gently to combine. Serve immediately.

Crab and Avocado Salad

Ingredients:

- 1 pound crab meat, cooked
- 2 ripe avocados, diced
- 1/2 cup cherry tomatoes, halved
- 1/4 cup red onion, finely chopped
- 2 tablespoons lime juice
- 2 tablespoons olive oil
- Salt and pepper, to taste

Instructions:

1. In a large bowl, gently combine crab meat, avocados, cherry tomatoes, and red onion.
2. Drizzle with lime juice and olive oil, then season with salt and pepper.
3. Toss gently to combine and serve immediately.

Farro Salad with Vegetables

Ingredients:

- 1 cup cooked farro
- 1 cup cherry tomatoes, halved
- 1/2 cucumber, diced
- 1/4 bell pepper, diced
- 1/4 cup parsley, chopped
- 3 tablespoons olive oil
- Juice of 1 lemon
- Salt and pepper, to taste

Instructions:

1. In a large bowl, combine cooked farro, cherry tomatoes, cucumber, bell pepper, and parsley.
2. Drizzle with olive oil and lemon juice, then season with salt and pepper.
3. Toss gently to combine and serve chilled or at room temperature.

Green Bean and Potato Salad

Ingredients:

- 1 pound green beans, trimmed
- 2 cups small potatoes, halved
- 1/4 cup red onion, finely chopped
- 1/4 cup fresh dill, chopped
- 3 tablespoons olive oil
- Juice of 1 lemon
- Salt and pepper, to taste

Instructions:

1. In a pot of boiling salted water, cook potatoes until tender, about 10 minutes. Add green beans and cook for an additional 4-5 minutes. Drain and let cool.
2. In a large bowl, combine potatoes, green beans, red onion, and dill.
3. Drizzle with olive oil and lemon juice, then season with salt and pepper. Toss to combine and serve chilled or at room temperature.

Cabbage Slaw with Apples

Ingredients:

- 4 cups green cabbage, shredded
- 1 cup carrots, grated
- 1 cup apple, julienned
- 1/4 cup raisins
- 1/4 cup apple cider vinegar
- 2 tablespoons honey
- 2 tablespoons olive oil
- Salt and pepper, to taste

Instructions:

1. In a large bowl, combine cabbage, carrots, apples, and raisins.
2. In a small bowl, whisk together apple cider vinegar, honey, olive oil, salt, and pepper.
3. Pour the dressing over the slaw and toss to combine. Serve immediately or refrigerate for 30 minutes before serving.

Tropical Fruit Salad

Ingredients:

- 2 cups pineapple, diced
- 2 cups mango, diced
- 2 cups kiwi, sliced
- 1 cup strawberries, sliced
- 1/4 cup mint leaves, chopped
- Juice of 1 lime

Instructions:

1. In a large bowl, combine pineapple, mango, kiwi, and strawberries.
2. Drizzle with lime juice and toss gently to combine.
3. Garnish with mint leaves and serve immediately.

Cucumber Dill Salad

Ingredients:

- 2 large cucumbers, sliced
- 1/4 cup red onion, thinly sliced
- 1/4 cup fresh dill, chopped
- 1/2 cup Greek yogurt
- 1 tablespoon lemon juice
- Salt and pepper, to taste

Instructions:

1. In a large bowl, combine cucumbers, red onion, and dill.
2. In a small bowl, mix Greek yogurt, lemon juice, salt, and pepper.
3. Pour the dressing over the cucumber mixture and toss gently to combine. Serve chilled.

Roasted Cauliflower Salad

Ingredients:

- 1 head cauliflower, cut into florets
- 2 tablespoons olive oil
- Salt and pepper, to taste
- 1/4 cup raisins
- 1/4 cup almonds, sliced
- 1/4 cup parsley, chopped
- 2 tablespoons lemon juice

Instructions:

1. Preheat the oven to 425°F (220°C). Toss cauliflower with olive oil, salt, and pepper, and spread on a baking sheet. Roast for 25-30 minutes until golden.
2. In a large bowl, combine roasted cauliflower, raisins, almonds, and parsley.
3. Drizzle with lemon juice and toss to combine. Serve warm or at room temperature.

Spinach and Goat Cheese Salad

Ingredients:

- 4 cups fresh spinach
- 1/4 cup goat cheese, crumbled
- 1/4 cup walnuts, toasted
- 1/2 cup strawberries, sliced
- 3 tablespoons balsamic vinaigrette

Instructions:

1. In a large bowl, combine spinach, goat cheese, walnuts, and strawberries.
2. Drizzle with balsamic vinaigrette and toss gently to combine. Serve immediately.

Grilled Peach Salad

Ingredients:

- 2 ripe peaches, halved and pitted
- 4 cups arugula
- 1/4 cup feta cheese, crumbled
- 1/4 cup walnuts, toasted
- 2 tablespoons balsamic glaze

Instructions:

1. Preheat the grill to medium heat. Grill peach halves for 2-3 minutes per side until slightly charred.
2. In a large bowl, combine arugula, grilled peaches, feta cheese, and walnuts.
3. Drizzle with balsamic glaze and toss gently to combine. Serve warm or at room temperature.

Apple Walnut Salad

Ingredients:

- 4 cups mixed greens
- 1 large apple, thinly sliced
- 1/4 cup walnuts, toasted
- 1/4 cup blue cheese, crumbled
- 3 tablespoons apple cider vinaigrette

Instructions:

1. In a large bowl, combine mixed greens, apple slices, walnuts, and blue cheese.
2. Drizzle with apple cider vinaigrette and toss gently to combine. Serve immediately.

Egg and Avocado Salad

Ingredients:

- 4 hard-boiled eggs, chopped
- 1 ripe avocado, diced
- 1/4 cup mayonnaise
- 1 tablespoon Dijon mustard
- Salt and pepper, to taste
- 2 tablespoons fresh chives, chopped

Instructions:

1. In a large bowl, combine eggs and avocado.
2. In a small bowl, mix mayonnaise, Dijon mustard, salt, and pepper.
3. Pour the dressing over the egg and avocado mixture, add chives, and toss gently to combine. Serve on toast or in a sandwich.

Panzanella Salad

Ingredients:

- 4 cups crusty bread, cubed
- 2 cups ripe tomatoes, chopped
- 1 cucumber, diced
- 1/4 cup red onion, thinly sliced
- 1/4 cup fresh basil, torn
- 3 tablespoons olive oil
- 2 tablespoons red wine vinegar
- Salt and pepper, to taste

Instructions:

1. Preheat the oven to 400°F (200°C). Toss bread cubes with olive oil, salt, and pepper, and bake for 10-15 minutes until golden.
2. In a large bowl, combine tomatoes, cucumber, red onion, basil, and toasted bread.
3. Drizzle with red wine vinegar and toss gently to combine. Serve immediately.

Creamy Coleslaw

Ingredients:

- 4 cups green cabbage, shredded
- 1 cup carrots, grated
- 1/2 cup mayonnaise
- 2 tablespoons apple cider vinegar
- 1 tablespoon sugar
- Salt and pepper, to taste

Instructions:

1. In a large bowl, combine cabbage and carrots.
2. In a small bowl, whisk together mayonnaise, apple cider vinegar, sugar, salt, and pepper.
3. Pour the dressing over the cabbage mixture and toss to combine. Refrigerate for at least 30 minutes before serving.

Italian Pasta Salad

Ingredients:

- 12 oz rotini pasta
- 1 cup cherry tomatoes, halved
- 1/2 cup black olives, sliced
- 1/2 cup mozzarella balls, halved
- 1/4 cup red onion, chopped
- 1/4 cup fresh basil, chopped
- 1/3 cup Italian dressing
- Salt and pepper, to taste

Instructions:

1. Cook pasta according to package instructions; drain and cool.
2. In a large bowl, combine cooled pasta, tomatoes, olives, mozzarella, onion, and basil.
3. Drizzle with Italian dressing, season with salt and pepper, and toss to combine. Serve chilled or at room temperature.

Mediterranean Orzo Salad

Ingredients:

- 1 cup orzo pasta
- 1 cup cherry tomatoes, halved
- 1/2 cup cucumber, diced
- 1/4 cup red onion, finely chopped
- 1/2 cup feta cheese, crumbled
- 1/4 cup kalamata olives, sliced
- 2 tablespoons olive oil
- 1 tablespoon lemon juice
- Salt and pepper, to taste

Instructions:

1. Cook orzo according to package instructions; drain and cool.
2. In a large bowl, combine orzo, tomatoes, cucumber, onion, feta, and olives.
3. Drizzle with olive oil and lemon juice, season with salt and pepper, and toss to combine. Serve chilled.

Cold Soba Noodle Salad

Ingredients:

- 8 oz soba noodles
- 1 cup carrots, julienned
- 1 cup red bell pepper, julienned
- 1/2 cup green onions, sliced
- 1/4 cup sesame seeds
- 1/4 cup soy sauce
- 2 tablespoons rice vinegar
- 1 tablespoon sesame oil
- Salt and pepper, to taste

Instructions:

1. Cook soba noodles according to package instructions; drain and cool.
2. In a large bowl, combine cooled noodles, carrots, bell pepper, green onions, and sesame seeds.
3. In a small bowl, whisk together soy sauce, rice vinegar, sesame oil, salt, and pepper. Pour over salad and toss to combine. Serve chilled.

Chickpea Tabbouleh

Ingredients:

- 1 cup bulgur wheat
- 1 can (15 oz) chickpeas, rinsed and drained
- 1 cup parsley, chopped
- 1/2 cup mint, chopped
- 1/2 cup tomatoes, diced
- 1/4 cup green onions, sliced
- 1/4 cup olive oil
- 3 tablespoons lemon juice
- Salt and pepper, to taste

Instructions:

1. Cook bulgur according to package instructions; let cool.
2. In a large bowl, combine cooked bulgur, chickpeas, parsley, mint, tomatoes, and green onions.
3. Drizzle with olive oil and lemon juice, season with salt and pepper, and toss to combine. Serve chilled.

Antipasto Salad

Ingredients:

- 4 cups mixed greens
- 1/2 cup salami, sliced
- 1/2 cup pepperoni, sliced
- 1/2 cup provolone cheese, cubed
- 1/4 cup black olives, sliced
- 1/4 cup artichoke hearts, quartered
- 1/4 cup roasted red peppers, sliced
- 1/3 cup Italian dressing

Instructions:

1. In a large bowl, layer mixed greens, salami, pepperoni, provolone, olives, artichokes, and roasted red peppers.
2. Drizzle with Italian dressing and toss gently to combine. Serve immediately.

Avocado and Bean Salad

Ingredients:

- 1 can (15 oz) black beans, rinsed and drained
- 1 can (15 oz) corn, drained
- 2 ripe avocados, diced
- 1/2 cup red onion, chopped
- 1/4 cup cilantro, chopped
- 1 lime, juiced
- Salt and pepper, to taste

Instructions:

1. In a large bowl, combine black beans, corn, avocados, red onion, and cilantro.
2. Drizzle with lime juice, season with salt and pepper, and toss gently to combine. Serve immediately.

Shrimp and Mango Salad

Ingredients:

- 1 lb shrimp, peeled and deveined
- 2 ripe mangoes, diced
- 1 red bell pepper, diced
- 1/4 cup red onion, chopped
- 1/4 cup cilantro, chopped
- 2 tablespoons lime juice
- Salt and pepper, to taste

Instructions:

1. In a skillet, cook shrimp over medium heat until pink and cooked through; let cool.
2. In a large bowl, combine shrimp, mangoes, bell pepper, onion, and cilantro.
3. Drizzle with lime juice, season with salt and pepper, and toss gently to combine. Serve chilled.

Quinoa and Black Bean Salad

Ingredients:

- 1 cup quinoa, cooked
- 1 can (15 oz) black beans, rinsed and drained
- 1 cup corn, drained
- 1 red bell pepper, diced
- 1/4 cup cilantro, chopped
- 1/4 cup lime juice
- 2 tablespoons olive oil
- Salt and pepper, to taste

Instructions:

1. In a large bowl, combine cooked quinoa, black beans, corn, bell pepper, and cilantro.
2. Drizzle with lime juice and olive oil, season with salt and pepper, and toss to combine. Serve chilled.

Sweet Potato and Kale Salad

Ingredients:

- 2 medium sweet potatoes, peeled and diced
- 1 bunch kale, chopped
- 1/2 cup quinoa, cooked
- 1/4 cup red onion, thinly sliced
- 1/4 cup dried cranberries
- 1/4 cup feta cheese, crumbled
- 3 tablespoons olive oil
- 2 tablespoons apple cider vinegar
- Salt and pepper, to taste

Instructions:

1. Preheat the oven to 400°F (200°C). Toss the sweet potatoes with olive oil, salt, and pepper on a baking sheet. Roast for 20-25 minutes or until tender.
2. In a large bowl, combine the kale, cooked quinoa, red onion, dried cranberries, and feta cheese.
3. Once the sweet potatoes are done, let them cool slightly, then add them to the salad.
4. Drizzle with apple cider vinegar, toss to combine, and serve warm or at room temperature.

Mediterranean Couscous Salad

Ingredients:

- 1 cup couscous
- 1 1/4 cups vegetable broth
- 1 cup cherry tomatoes, halved
- 1/2 cup cucumber, diced
- 1/4 cup red onion, finely chopped
- 1/4 cup kalamata olives, sliced
- 1/2 cup feta cheese, crumbled
- 1/4 cup fresh parsley, chopped
- 3 tablespoons olive oil
- 2 tablespoons lemon juice
- Salt and pepper, to taste

Instructions:

1. In a saucepan, bring the vegetable broth to a boil. Stir in the couscous, cover, and remove from heat. Let it sit for 5 minutes, then fluff with a fork.
2. In a large bowl, combine the cooked couscous, cherry tomatoes, cucumber, red onion, olives, feta cheese, and parsley.
3. Drizzle with olive oil and lemon juice, season with salt and pepper, and toss to combine. Serve chilled or at room temperature.